ALSO BY JAMES KOLLER

Two Hands, Poems, 1959-1961, 1965
Brainard & Washington Street Poems, 1965
The Dogs & Other Dark Woods, 1966
Some Cows, Poems of Civilization & Domestic Life, 1965
I Went to See My True Love, 1967
California Poems, 1971
Messages, 1972
If You Don't Like Me You Can Leave Me Alone, 1974
Shannon, Who Was Lost Before, 1975
Bureau Creek, 1975

POEMS FOR THE BLUE SKY

JAMES KOLLER

BLACK
SPARROW
PRESS
SANTA BARBARA
1976

POEMS FOR THE BLUE SKY. Copyright © 1976 by James Koller. All rights reserved. Printed in the United States of America. No part of this book may be used or reproduced in any manner whatsoever without written permission except in the case of brief quotations embodied in critical articles and reviews. For information address Black Sparrow Press, P.O. Box 3993, Santa Barbara, CA 93105.

ACKNOWLEDGEMENT

Most of the poems included here were selected from the following books:

Two Hands, Poems 1959-1961, Seattle, 1965.
The Dogs & Other Dark Woods, San Francisco, 1966.
Some Cows, Poems of Civilization & Domestic Life,
    San Francisco, 1966.
California Poems, Los Angeles, 1971.

Other poems appeared in *Alcheringa, Coyote's Journal, San Francisco Oracle,* and *The Yale Review,* to whose editors grateful acknowledgment is made.

Message first appeared in a pamphlet published by the Institute of Further Studies, Buffalo, 1972.

LIBRARY OF CONGRESS CATALOGING IN PUBLICATION DATA

Koller, James.
  Poems for the blue sky.

  I. Title.
PS3561.04A17   1976   811'.5'4   76-22616
ISBN 0-87685-258-4
ISBN 0-87685-257-6 pbk.

CONTENTS

I

MESSAGE IN MY POEMS   9

II
(1959-1963)

"cut the ground pick & axe the frozen ground"	15
"I have cut an eagle"	17
"fingers smeared green & blue"	19
"green green green your eyes"	20
THE BIRTH / AUGUST 21, 1960	21
"mottled brown birds"	23
"the hard metal of her teeth"	25
"in water in water in water"	27
"I AM MYSELF A WALL IN DARK RAIN"	30
"O WITH AN AXE AN AXE I BUILD WITH AN AXE"	31
THREE POEMS FOR ERNEST HEMINGWAY	32
"FOR FOUR HOURS SHE HAS EATEN PLACENTA"	36
"BUILD WITH AN AXE"	38
SOME MAGIC	39

III
(1963-1967)

"my grandfather, who was also Irish"	45
"HOW MANY MAGGOTS IN WHOSE BRAIN???"	46
"O DIRTY BIRD YR GIZZARD'S TOO BIG & FULL OF SAND"	49
"DID YOU EVER WONDER WHY SO MANY PEOPLE DON'T HAVE CHILDREN???"	52
"salt water swirls at the stone"	54
"Well, if it ain't old Wolf Tit"	55
SNOW ON MOUNT SAINT HELENA	59

IV
(1967-1970)

WOLF SONGS & Other Songs of the Tlinget	63
SONGS OF THE TETON SIOUX	68
CROW SONG	80
"We change to keep all else the same"	83
"Mars, opalescent orange, McIbbon's crystal ball"	84
"the deer, out of the trees, downhill"	86
"All through the night they rode"	87
WIND / Fragments for a beginning	89

I

MESSAGE IN MY POEMS

Sign is the stimulus for vision and message. What for me connotes worthwhile sign usually falls into the category of animal or natural, and usually the sign will reside in my mind over a period of time while it accumulates other signs—sort of like a magnet might draw certain metals to it. These signs combine to create a vision. In writing down the vision I will begin to consider the message to me, and whatever message the poem finally has is that message. How I make it work is not to talk about the message, but to relate the signs as they were—or as they fit into the final message. Often there are signs that don't enhance a particular message or vision, and these signs get lost somewhere along the way. In other words, you have in the final poem a vision which must generalize itself into a message.

An instance of sign: I might see a flock of crows flying in some particular direction. If there is no apparent reason for their flight, or for their direction, I will be aware of the phenomenon as sign. I won't know of what, but I'll carry the image until it multiplies into several images. If I've seen crows flying north, I will be tuned to north and anything out of north or that relates to it in any way for me is likely to attach itself in my mind to the image of crows. Finally the images will have congregated to the point that I'll have a sense of knowing something I didn't know before. I'll write them down and when I see them written they will generalize themselves into a meaning and that meaning becomes message and is different from any one sign. It might be inherent in the signs—will be—but is more than the signs themselves.

The natural relationships of animals and birds will obviously enter into the signs they give me. In other words, I am not laying out a message—it evolves from the stimulus. It evolves to a point where I sense its presence. I think nearly always I am hard put to tell you exactly what the message might be, but I think that the images which make me feel that I've gotten something from them will make others feel the same way. I think there is communication between things of an unlike nature. I think for instance that birds can communicate with people. Animals can and will communicate even more—especially wild animals. I think that places—configurations of rocks and trees and water in place—have at least auras which are meaningful. I don't think they're accidentally meaningful. Anything with aura has personae who come like the personae of persons you meet.

The sense of message comes from an awareness of personae and the communication between the personae and yourself.

The nature of an animal or bird stays in his parts. The wings of a crow, the claws of an owl speak at least owlness and crowness. Pound said that the poet was the antenna of his race. I think that poetry has to deal with the gods—whatever gods there are. Good poetry is a message from the gods. If I see signs that come from nature—which are generally the only signs I personally see—the gods I'm concerned with are natural gods. (Maybe they're not gods, maybe they're spirits, maybe they're ghosts, maybe they were people but they're not people anymore but ghostpeople, or maybe they are people, people in some sort of frenzy that separates them from the usual or enhances the usual. It's these people that give messages.)

Things fashioned by man from nature, or things made by man and worked on by nature have spirits. Anything has spirits if they're willing to let you know they're there.

When I begin a poem I'm looking for the message, what the spirits have to say to me. Once I have the sense of the message I can try to focus the message.

I see poetry as a celebration—a celebration of everything that exists, is alive, or has been alive (in any sense of the word). For me a good poem is one that has in it enough spirits that I know what's going on, what's being celebrated. The spirits tell me what's being celebrated. I once saw a cow with a placenta still hanging from it, a calf lying on the ground beside the cow. All by themselves they were the celebration of birth. Above the cow and the calf there were crows and hawks circling. With death hanging over them the cow and calf became a celebration of the whole thing, the thin balance that life is.

I present what has shown itself to me, then acknowledge what I've found. I acknowledge signs and by presenting themselves they generalize, make a story, give a message, whatever story or message that these particular spirits want told or given. In a way it's as though I'm a door for the spirits to walk through, or a mouth for the spirits to talk through. I suppose you could say that my role as poet is little different from a naturalist's, except that he sees feathers or skins where I see spirits. I'm recording phenomena that appear to and through me. I don't really think that I have any message, but that the message gives itself through what has shown itself to me. I think that anything really considered a message has to come that way. If someone has something that they consciously want to tell someone else it won't come across in the same way. The poet gets in the way. The poet doesn't let the thing talk for itself. He comes with a preconceived idea and that's the idea he puts down. His idea is message and any images are there only to prove his point. It's all in how it comes through you. If you have a preconceived notion it won't work. You have to give the place, the spirits. They have to do their own talking. When someone tells you about something you're getting his idea of it, you don't know what he really saw. You have only the message he wanted to give you. You have to give the spirits, not what you think of them.

Sometimes you can go on from all this. If the spirits are really with you and you know what it is they're saying, you can talk back, converse with them. This is the hardest thing to do, because you're likely to lose them and you won't have anything. But if you can get what they're saying, and if you can talk to them, and you're where they're at, you've gone as far as you need to go.

II
(1959-1963)

cut the ground pick & axe the frozen ground
shovel lumps of coal into the holes
burn them & dig deeper

I smile into your small eyes
through steam see you my green eyes come orange & red
hang on you smiling

owls shot feathered snow
dropping on your head
the rat dead in a pine box
beat with a shovel

I smile

the sky gray rain
I come out cold look around

the sun will shine
bears & lonely grasses rubbing tree trunks

the pine scrub
I cold
stone I smile

summer will be blue mountain goats
flowers all over the slopes

the pine box burns

smoke out my ears
snapping jumping red dogs licking my legs

I smile green eyes

smoke in your small eyes

chipmunks beg coyote food in the rain
run on my head yipping

the pine chairs of fall the wood squeaking
thunder showers
& fire will roll up in blankets

I have cut an eagle
from wood
& he is a man I am a man
a starved thin dog an eagle a coyote
in a corner

no one will cut off my ears

I nose leaves & grass
on ridges where I run rabbits & mice
I sniff the air

I see a bearded hunter
he follows after me
long arms long rifle

I sit where he cannot see

across the creek before him
my ears are my own

I cover his eyes beat at his eyes
with wings talons splinter-sharp teeth
in his shoulders rip his legs

I pull him down
pull him down
run away

YAK YAK YAK

I hide & watch
he will never find my wooden legs

fingers smeared green & blue
eyes pouring salt

rubbed into the skin

well-chewed skin hairless
in an indian woman's short teeth

urine tanned legs
dribbling old men scratch their heads
one sailor to another sick in the hold
no life on the wall
hung up
on the wall

chewed & hung out
dried stretched empty
fishnets on fingers
worked over

blood all over the hair drum
the pearl an egg on your finger

o I will beat the drum
thump the drum
o my fingers bleed
break through
up between your arms
the blue egg
the broken blue egg

green green green your eyes
you lay in an old tree
scratching your leg

I will cut your skin from you
pour your blood over me
I will wear your skin look out your eyes
hot with blood
you stick to me stick to me dark red

I curl in the sun
stretch & yawn
climb down & roll in pine needles & grass
my dark body

my eyes green green green my eyes

THE BIRTH / AUGUST 21, 1960

looking out the blind looking
I have never been never
before the wind rattles
my doors are people all around
open windows with dog's blood
red in their hair
yellow & red the smell walks
through the room & sticks
the heads in bottles I am tailed
with feathers & rattles
hang my hands o green
my eyes snake through

to carry down white horses carry
out my shirt black & red to my belt
I wear black rage & red
o out by morning
through the streets red
ran through the streets by morning
I wake in the morning you
awake can you hear the dogs
all around you can they come
this spring pass over the bridge
& down & down the straights

dark the slant sprung eyes the womb
dark o black your hair born & red
the dogs run & fall
out of this never the building will

fall can you
see me throw my legs bend the stick
the windows bend & close
the light the white
to bed I climb go good night
to bed white horses
feathered their heads
poke poke into the bottles
their ears in your hair
let down your hair & sleep

o burn all smoke the mountains
fire winters all
cover my stick with blindness
out by morning the fires
shout o rattle the window's voices
the heads glass the shouts curses drop
roll away I roll winter away o white
& red the head that bleeds the shirt
blood stumbles down through the stairs
go blind the dogs born
blind they speak & born speak fire
yellow & red the morning streets all green
my eyes blind the young

mottled brown birds
with hooked mouths

they hide in the grass

& I step among them
    their wings beat at the sun

    & rain

    & fox squats on the grass
    with open mouth
    making sounds with tongue in teeth

    a wing thrown against me
    into my eyes

o they swing back & forth
over my head

    hands

    & fox sits
    at the end of the track
    while the ties turn green
    & grow into the ground

        & his tongue in his teeth
        makes sounds

       & the sun was round once

o the wing thrown into my eyes

    reached into the fox's mouth
    back along his tongue

       to his belly

the hard metal of her teeth
silver mouth

& she grins

I go down to her river
which is blood
& drown myself in my own sperm

        the raccoon watches
        & covers his eyes

  sail on your own waters
  sail on
      your own

I bury my blade silver in the door
the old half sprung door

    o the sail is half gone
    blood all over me

    I smear it on my face
    & beat the drums of her belly

    ten men on a hill
    poplar shaking hands with the wind

        & the raccoon won't eat
        covers his eyes

with a silver knife
buried & twisting the door

& the sun in her hair is not so bright
her teeth are brighter

        o the raccoons
        each in tree
        poplar
        close their eyes

  o the wind blows flowers over her
  o the rain beads on her belly
     pools on her belly

& the moon is full a sail furled & jammed into the night
   the menstrual night

        & I pull I pull down
                down

o the blood is rain & blots out the poplars
shivering silver in my door

       & the raccoons
       the raccoons
               have no eyes

in water in water in water
I float down

my eyes open my eyes open

    & great horses black & red
    fuck in the fields

my eyes are open

& I watch the horses
by green & white light

        & MY EYES FLOAT FROM ME

        & THE HORSES BY STORM
        IN MUD
        LARGE MY HANDS & HANDS
        OVER THEM

        LARGE IN MUD
        & LIGHTNING
        LIGHTNING

        FIRE MY FINGERS ON FIRE

        MY HANDS

  the horses   black and red   in mud
  & I   in mud

& MY HANDS

down to the river
& into the river

I walk to my knees in water
    to my shoulders

    & the water covers me over

& my eyes
  my eyes

        BLACK & RED
       THE HORSES BURN

        & I TOUCH HER

      MY HANDS OVER HER

       BANKS ON FIRE

        THE HORSES
         FIRE

       & INTO THE AIR

around me water
my hands reach up through water

      DRY BY FIRE

& green eyes look down
& up through water

& her back is down

   & sleek

   her tongue cold

   O UNDER MY BELLY MY BELLY MY BELLY
          COVERED WITH WATER

   O EYES OVER HER O & WITHIN HER WITHIN HER

     & THE HORSES COME TO DRINK

I AM MYSELF A WALL IN DARK RAIN
blurred & shifting as the light
around me

not clearly defined there is no impact
the wall moving is adrift

BUT DEFINITION IS LIMITATION & I
am without bounds
                 no skin
IN DARK RAIN WHICH IS NOWHERE WHICH IS NO
definition

I AM WATER WORN ON A DARK WINDOW AGAINST
darker rain

        the wind my will

O WITH AN AXE AN AXE I BUILD WITH AN AXE

the birds are brown & brown the branches
the branches & the birds sing in the wind
& I sing just as loud

I BUILD WITH AN AXE SET FREE THE BIRDS
the branches in the wind fall far

I BUILD FOR BURNING FOR BURNING

a living tree stripped for burning
green green green a post remains

    I AM THAT POST A POST OF FIRE

    o on a empty plain

    filling the wind with green
    my green smoke
               my arms folded

THREE POEMS FOR
ERNEST HEMINGWAY

1.

THE HAWK SWING THE BLOOD BLOOD THE ACT
& HOW MUCH   HOW FAR   HOW CLOSE
    BEFORE THE FIRE CATCHES

THE HAIR   THE SKIN   THE BLOOD

    & the bone

MEASURE   the nearness

the coming together
close in
the contact   explosion
& flow   the blood

& ALL THIS LITTLE BEARING ON WHAT OR
WHERE   ALTOGETHER VERY LITTLE

    how   is of importance

the hawk
the motion of him
the swing   not small
an arc   of light

the tempo of light
& color   IN BLACKNESS

THE HAWK BECAUSE HE MOVES
AWAY FROM IT &   INTO IT

the pulsing   the pump   the blood
that comes   that goes
                          the blood

the fact of it
the act   the movement

    ABOVE ALL ELSE

the hawk
is alive   & I

but how long   the measure

the sense of it
the only sense

    THE FIRE WHICH BURNS ME

    THE HAWK EXPLODING

the only way to travel

2.

THE TEETH CLOSE THE BONE SMASHED THE BONE
SPLINTERS

& the thing accomplished quickly
no reflection

ANIMAL DEATH

there is no time
for reason
to the right or to the left
THERE IS TIME TO ACT ONLY

THE HEAD IS MOUTH FOR STOMACH & HUNGER

    there is nothing more   more or less
    a little a long way

& THE IMPORTANCE OF ACTION
best observed in the dead
the bones broken
life sticking splinters & blood
through the skin
not quick enough

the readiness of the hand   the jaw

nothing more

EVEN IN LOVE

3.

I USE MY FINGERS FIND THE PASSAGE THE ENTRY &
ENTER   GO IN   CLOSE THE FLAPS BEHIND ME
I am in   over my head   (that
of importance

but the movement
THE IMMERSION
AS ACTION
most important)

I move deeply   water in my ears my eyes my nose
move   within   move   my mouth

I carry it around me
& not folded

cold   move into it
within   I warm

THE MOVEMENT   BLOOD
KEEPING ME
MAKING IT
MOVEMENT   now you see him now you don't
                like that

            & MOVING   MY HANDS BEFORE ME
        FEELING OF EVERYTHING

(she is with child

& I am not alone
but separate)
ALL MOTION

A BIRTH   in the ground
            the dogs don't bark
            at you
            your tent

FOR FOUR HOURS SHE HAS EATEN PLACENTA
six placentas in four hours the sacks
broken the water
drained the blind pups six times out
on their bellies their legs drag behind
like fish to the breasts & the tongue
dries their breath & finally
the bodies sleep seven
sleep mama & six pups who are
WHAT IT IS ALL ABOUT WHAT SHE
is here for we
are here for the breeding the breath
the young who chew blind
mouths the breasts
their mothers our women
are for breeding & life
FOR THE LIVING THE GIVING OF IT
the narrow motion the passage
the fluid fuck the breath of it
for breeding & the blood that flows
through us the food
FOR DEATH IS EVERYWHERE IS CONSTANT & PRESENT &
looking after us not to be forgotten
we are not & death is not & life
moves us & death too
moves us & after us breeding we are
breeding & life is for the living and death
is for the living
not to be buried

DEATH WITH HIS JAWS OPEN THE MEAT
torn on his tongue red the
father hunting the father anxious
to kill for love the movement the process
the fluids dropping from her the red &
after the birth red & she is all
teeth & growls & life & death
& love the food
the fluids between them

BUILD WITH AN AXE
cut the dead away the leaners
drop them down onto the ground   crash
them down   build a pyre a tower
a large based pyramid   for burning
the leaners the dead weight the hanging
on   & maybe the trees left
will come down too the soil is so
shallow   but LET THOSE STANDING ALONE
have the chance   to put out their roots
to dig in   & grow
what it's all about   why we cut &
burn   we burn to KEEP ALIVE

all about you the dead & the leaning
you cut too what
it's all about   or
you fall too

SOME MAGIC

for Don Allen

I AM ALL THINGS. The grizzlies if I ain't
loud enough. He was an old man. THEY COME
THEY COME. The gray the white. They come
along side of the herds. The crippled the young
& their wolves. LIFE IS VERY DANGEROUS.
Until over. The hungry know. The sick the
lame. The herds are thinned. Nothing eats
too lame to procreate. He came to me one of
the lined his beard white his life very dangerous.
Won't be the same after you go. IT'S ALL IN
THE TREES. THERE IN THE ROCK. IN THE
AIR BENEATH THE ICE. To breathe. I can
tell you stories. Understand. He had no teeth.

ALL WOULD TURN YOU TO YOUR OWN DARK WOODS.
I can go anywhere do anything. I am myself
but I am also all else. Order. Within me.
Keeps the wind. I am in the snow. I can grow
into anything. I am caribou the wolf is one
with me. WE ARE HUNGERED FOR. HUNGRY.
There is no well-being. EAT. ONE GRUNTS
FOR ALL ELSE. The caribou is the wolf's
paw. I MOVE TO CHANGE TO FILL MYSELF.
Old man.

His teeth worn away. White snow gray down
to the old. HAVE NO CONTROL. Be filled.
Sick & young. Food. His face dark as shale.
Old man. Before you take a look before you.

Rock where now there are dead. Order.
Within all things sharp cliffs. Because they are
hungry and hunger rules. The wind will blow
me snow cover me. I know only what I am as
I enter into it as it numbs my feet. Go if you
have never been. Burn neither hoof nor tongue.

You are kin. The same mountain. Come up.
The wolf is ever there. They are one before
me. The snow fresh on my feet. I can neither
lie nor stand. The shape I am. I can tell
you many. IF YOU ARE KIN.

I AM THE SUN COME I AM THE SUN & STAND
MY GROUND I AM HIGH. They come over shale
splinter cliffs caribou come wolves run thin
the herds bring down the slow runners. There
are those who live no barriers. Their stomachs
old inexperienced. Thin the herds that the
healthy may go on. Not too many young or old.
The old man long beard no teeth. It is all
here if you've never been here. If you don't
do anything. Where there are trees. In the
rivers. Under the ice between the river &
the ice. Find a hole to come up the old man
said. I counted teeth.

NEEDS THAT ARE NOT YOUR OWN. Go. When
the way becomes all things. There is no
blowing me away I find my way out into the storm.
I AM A TREE SHALE ONE WITH ALL THINGS.
THE SAME. ONE & THE SAME. I do not lay
flat. The shale cuts at my air. As I come
to it. Between the rivers look around. ALL
IS ONE & ALL IS PART. THE CARIBOU FLANK
& THE WOLF STOMACH. The same river runs

through all dark woods. THE HUNGRY AND
THE HUNGERED FOR. The ground is one with
those who stand & those who move. TO FILL
THE WORLD I AM IN THAT IS IN ME. Stories
he said. He was a wolf. I can't hear you.
Too much water. Kin. For the big breakup.
On high ground.

III
(1963-1967)

my grandfather, who was also Irish
& had the nose for it, said he was part Red Man

my mother, his daughter, is English

   & don't you bring home any Indian girls

when the man died, they stretched his body in a tree
this out of Browning, Montana

   against the law, the White Man said
   we don't want to see any more bodies in trees
   you bury them, like everybody else

the Hawk has an Indian nose

     Crow is black because he stole fire

     he learned from everybody he ever stole from

     Coyote is the color of his own dried blood

HOW MANY MAGGOTS IN WHOSE BRAIN???

they were huckleberries in my belly

    can't keep it straight
      all the time

what are you doing in there?

    come in & see

            I can try
            can't I?

he stood two legs up
his ears & eyes moss over the rock
watched as we tracked him

        we couldn't keep up

finally we spotted him
a mile down wind
we knew we'd never hit him

stole everything he could get his teeth in

    o, I'd never, not me
    to get caught, is the crime

        she crossed her legs

they were sisters, two agreed
& I listened to the other
who thought as I did

              was always right

after I made the world
I put people on it

& that was the most fun

      did you ever make anybody???

"when in a new & strange situation
    do nothing"

to get caught is the crime

"when in a new & strange situation
    escape"

        you can try
        can't you?

    try me, she said
    & turned to stone

    I rolled her into the river

where do we go from here?

    she had a ball of fat in her mouth

    she still has
    a ball of fat
    in her mouth

a hell of a lot of good it's going to do her

O DIRTY BIRD YR GIZZARD'S TOO BIG & FULL OF SAND

      he knew what I wanted
      wouldn't leave his spring
      I told him I'd sleep there with him
      & when he was sleeping soundly
      I went outside found dog droppings

      Ganuk, Ganuk, wake up
      you've shit in yr blankets

      he went out & I drank the spring

this the fellow
made the world

      got the birds together

      who can fly into the bear's asshole?

      wren did it

      came out with the bear's intestines

      the bear's end
                   he ate it

this the fellow
made the world
                   in certain circles

Caw Caw Caw

when bears go inside
they take off their coats
look like everybody else

"Do you speak English?"

              in circles

Caw Caw Caw

"I speak American."

    Samuel Colt patented his revolver in 1836

    Abraham Lincoln pushed its production
      twenty-some years later

    mass production
    mass reduction

"I knew there was something wrong with you."

  he came to a bunch of boys
  throwing fat at one another

  he jeered at them
  they threw fat at him
    he ate it

  & threw dog droppings at the boys
  they threw fat at him

    he ate it

threw more dog droppings at them
& they threw fat

    it's still the same game

this the fellow
made the world

    what it is

DID YOU EVER WONDER WHY SO MANY PEOPLE DON'T HAVE CHILDREN???

he cried too much
we called the land-otter-man
Djinakaxwats!a fed the boy

    what looked to be blackberries

"Let's go & take a sweat bath"

    poor little head

we found him two days later
deep in the wood   with a big belly

DO NOT SWALLOW THE SAP. YOU MIGHT HAVE A BABY

not crying nearly so loud

    we knew something was wrong
boiled up a dried salmon broth

    the heat made the little creatures come out
spiders ran from his mouth ears nose eyes buttocks
    they had eaten all but his skin

    which we threw away

"after they have loved each other for a while fall out"

salt water swirls at the stone
sandstone, an alcove's gentle curves
ridges & hollows, a honey-combed holy place
where I led my daughter, almost a cave
at the water's edge. we sat on our heels
the tide in, caressed the stone
this is the owl's house, she said

"Well, if it ain't old Wolf Tit"

I ain't no Shanshiro Sugata
   smiling in my sleep—
the crazy one taking his knife from my throat
   chewing his nails in fear

      "I'm in on something—
        this ain't no one night stand"

     but my eyes are open

why do you walk so fast?

  a lope
    (can't walk a straight line
      unless I walk fast)

  the secret is out

"It is a heavy load—
  they all are"

  put in hot water, a toilet
    Kyoto, settling in

      an old roommate returning

I bought another bottle

(visitors from the north)
Inventory: 1 gallon red wine—Paisano
11 12 oz. bottles of beer—Budweiser
⅕ gallon sake—Koshu
⅕ gallon bourbon—Jack Daniels
⅕ gallon rye—Old Overholt

(Ed & Carole, Vanny, Paula, Nico & Philip)
   settling in

& tea: Darjeeling, Lapsang Suchong, Oolong, Gen-mai

   all cups full

the wolf looks after his family

   I'm looking

   wind warnings in the Siskiyou
   snow down to 2,000 feet in the Sierra
   nine inches of rain San Bernardino County
     where one & a half is usual
     floods, slides

     all is not usual

IT ALL HAS TO DO WITH THE ANIMAL—THE MEAT BLOOD
   BONE & HAIR
 IT'S ALL THERE—THE IMPACT

     whether or not we touch—
    I mean I don't have to touch you
     to know you are there

"There is a weapon in the room"

TO KNOW
    you only have to be there

groves of cedar, fir, oak—rock—running or standing
    water—mountains, plains, river valleys—
        snow & rain—the sun

you only have to be there

        flowers opening in your head

I ain't the mother of any civilization

    (the father of one girl-child—
    but you have to start somewhere)

I don't know anything until I get there

        "thin-chested?"

        "WOLF MAN!"

      I was always a gray wolf
      like Pere Vidal of Old

    looking after the chickens

save your silver bullets

    I lope
    in loops—circles

      (miles & miles—but circles)
          LE LOUP

like the 'white bear'
sometimes a grizzly phenomenon

IF MY HEART IS WITH YOU
it is because you were here
     with me

                (I felt her heart
                the pounding
                in the ground
                in the bottoms of my feet)

you know or you don't
   it's like that
& you do or you don't
   like that

        settle in

how did you know?
   my totem?

CANIS LUPIS
          didn't know it showed

SNOW ON MOUNT SAINT HELENA

the mountain behind me, I drove south & west
passed three Angels in Valley Ford
five more & a girl at the crossroads to Tomales
& four gassed up at Point Reyes Station, roared away
chrome & hair catching sunlight, to the north
to join the others

Billy & Toby were off, again
to Oregon, as per
I Ching, The Book of Changes

going thru changes

like music

harmoniously, minor discords
like she burned or threw away everything, always
burns her bridges
pulled the old light out of the ceiling
tore the wires loose, all connections

change gears

Angels at every turn
all crossed roads

both sides, the streets lined with Harleys, choppers
of every description

he opened her coat
& holding it open
carefully & with expert eye
examined
what she had to offer
so to speak, as it were

                                            a whole world
& nothing ever dies, it's all here
on every road, behind every tree
growing out of the ground, a beautiful
fire, flames

                I'm grinning

exhaust, carbon

                diamonds & threads
my mind is filled with diamonds & threads

we go off in all directions, thru intersections & crossed roads

a necklace to live in

IV
(1967-1970)

WOLF SONGS & Other Songs of the Tlinget
(after John R. Swanton)

o

I keep dreaming I'm dead
keep feeling like I'm home

o

SHAMAN SONG

I don't have any place to come up through
think I'll go to Chillkat come up there
I'll come up over there, & cry

o

Throw him into the river
let him float down
Crow can fish him out
downstream

o

HOW TO GET GRIZZLY SPIRIT

Come out of your body among us & we're all one
(we drop grease into the fire, before the grizzly's head
Whu Whu Whu is what we all say)

o

CRADLE SONGS

1.
I'm gonna marry my brother's wife
after he dies

2.
I like to crawl around the house after my brother's wife
I thought he might get up out of his grave & I was worried
I always follow her around town

3.
If I don't take anything to the party I'll feel bad
Little girls have to take something to a party or they'll feel bad
All you little girls better listen

4.
I'll shoot a little bird for little brother
I'll spear a little trout for little sister

o

FUNERAL SONG

You're like a drifting log with iron nails in it
I built my house from that log
I hope you float in like that log did
on a good sandy beach
The sun goes into the clouds
like you go into our great mother
That's why the world is so dark

o

That's a rich man coming
keep your feelings to yourself

o

We've all been invited up to Killisnoo
all us high bred people are going to eat together

o

How is it all gonna turn out
people on crow's river going up to wolf's town
I don't have any bad feelings about the crow people
never said anything at all about the wolf's children
if they'd come by I'd shake all their hands

o

I wonder what eagle did to him
all those crows around him
it only took one crow to make the world

o

I think about you & it's like having spirits come down on me
where is it that we were going to die together
don't you think you ought to do like you say

o

I know how people get treated when they die
I'm gonna have a good time, a lot to drink

o

You surprise me, crow
whenever you see wolf people
you get way up on some branch

o

I'm gonna die & won't see you all anymore
it doesn't matter that I'll lose lots of property
it's only what's gonna happen to me that I'm crying about

o

SONG FOR THE RICHEST WOMAN IN WRANGELL

I used to make fun of you when you were a little girl & poor
where do you get all your whiskey & why aren't you ashamed

o

SONG ON THE WAY TO JAIL

They sound like howling wolves from here
everybody just beginning to get drunk
& I have to go away

o

I don't know why you tell me I'm drunk
it's you been giving me all that whiskey

o

It's only whiskey that makes you pity me
what would it take to make you love me

o

My wife went away, left me
& like somebody who needs a good drink
I can't sleep

o

When an eagle takes a crow
he takes her for amusement

o

If you'd died I would've cut off my hair
I love you so much I would've blackened my face

o

Before he died
I saw his ghost

o

It would be very easy to die with a wolf woman
it would be very pleasant

o

He followed his own mind
got himself killed
can't blame anybody else

o

SONGS OF THE TETON SIOUX
(after Frances Densmore)

o

He was an old wolf, no teeth, his tail all but
bare. The war party thought he was one of
them, singing with a young man's voice, until
they saw him. He lay beside their fire, and
they cut up their best buffalo meat for him,
fed it to him. He taught them this song, and
always since they carry their medicine in
a wolfskin bag.

With powers you know nothing about
I made them come to life
with powers you cannot understand
I made them walk

Wolf people

With spirit powers
I made them walk
with spirit powers
I made them walk
with spirit powers
I made them walk
with spirit powers
I made them walk

o

Everybody was there, but they heard somebody singing. One of them climbed the hill and looked over. A wolf was sitting there, looking far off, and singing. The war party learned his song.

At daybreak
I go
I gallop
I go

At daybreak
I go
I trot
I go

At daybreak
I go
timidly
I go

At daybreak
I go
cautiously
I go

o

I dreamed I came to a wolf den. Only the little wolves were there. They were singing this song.

Father is away somewhere
will come home howling

Mother is away somewhere
will come home howling

69

Father is away somewhere
a buffalo calf in his belly

Mother is away somewhere
will come home howling

Now she returns
in a sacred manner she returns

o

Well, they were
supposed to come
& come they did
—they're there

See if you can find
what's left of them
see if you can find
what's left of them

o

I thought I was a wolf
but the owls are hooting
& I'm afraid of the dark

I thought I was a wolf
but I'm so hungry
I'm tired from just standing

I am a wolf
I go to many places
I'm just tired of that one

o

In wild flight
I sent the swallows
in wild flight
I made them go
in wild flight
before the clouds were gathered

In wild flight
I sent my horse
in wild flight
a swallow flying running
in wild flight
before the clouds were gathered

o

Owls hoot at me
owls hoot at me
I know what it's all about
I've heard them before

Wolves howl at me
wolves howl at me
I know what it's all about
I've heard them before

o

Deer are coming
red meat
coming
see them come

Eagles are coming
blue sky
coming
see them come

o

Send word, bear father
send word, bear father
I'm having a hard time
send word, bear father
I'm having a bad time

o

My paw is holy
herbs are everywhere
my paw
herbs are everywhere

My paw is holy
everything is holy
my paw
everything is holy

o

Whoever
thinks himself beautiful after
seeing me
has no heart

o

I am an elk
I am
I'm living
I'm living
a short life
I am

o

I thought I saw buffalo
& called out
I thought I saw buffalo
& called out
let them be buffalo

They were blackbirds
I walked toward them
& they were blackbirds

I thought I saw buffalo
& called out
I thought I saw buffalo
& called out
let them be buffalo

They were swallows
I walked toward them
& they were swallows

o

Now, right now
my voice makes everybody
tremble

O my enemy
sits asking for medicine
& he trembles

O he trembles
my voice makes everybody
tremble

o

He comes from the north
he comes to fight
he comes from the north
see him there

I throw dust on me
it changes me
I am a bear
when I go to meet him

o

You ran from the soldiers
Even the eagle dies

o

They come from all around
flying

The wind blows down from the north

Rattling to earth, flying
they come

They come from all around
they come

o

My horse flies along
I wear blue earth & brown
I make myself fly along
I make my horse fly along
I make myself fly along
I have done it

o

The sun is my friend
the sun is my friend
I wear a hoop
eagle feathers fastened to it—
the bird of day

The moon is my friend
the moon is my friend
I wear a crane & a hawk—
one the bird of night
the other sure with his prey

o

Here I am
look at me
I am the sun
look at me

Here I am
look at me
I am the moon
look at me

o

Where the wind blows
where the wind roars
I stand
from the west
the wind blows
the wind roars
I stand

o

At night
I move against the wind
I move
at night
I move
the owl hoots
I move

At dawn
I move against the wind
I move
at dawn
I move
the crow calls
I move

o

One who I
pretend to be
stands at the place
where I make him stand

One who I
pretend to be
stands at the place
where I make him stand

The man I
pretend to be
stands at the place
where I make him stand

One who I
pretend to be
stands at the place
where I make him stand

o

Way up north
where the wind blows
they are walking

Way up north
where the hail beats down the grass
they are walking

Way up north
in all that weather
they are walking

o

How to catch buffalo when you're starving.

Mention the pipe
white buffalo maiden brought it
as they walked they mentioned it
I have offered it
many times
as I walked

Mention red earth
as they walked they mentioned it
I have put it on me
many times
as I walked

Mention blue earth
as they walked they mentioned it
I have put it on me
many times
as I walked

o

Why do you come around
when I came to see you
you cried

o

All that fighting—
you should give it up
you should settle down
stop for good

o

When I was courting
they told me
I had no horses
so I'm looking

Crow, Crow
watch your horses
they say I'm a horse thief

Keep your eyes open
I'm wandering around anyway
I might as well look for horses

Night is different
than day
may my horses be many
o

Big Sister
come out come out
I bring back horses

Big Sister
come out come out
you may catch one
o

Whenever you went
after anything
you said Long Buffalo
was out in front

He lies over there

He lies over there
o

As the young men go by
I look for him
I always look for him
& he has gone
I will always look for him
& he has gone
  o

a wa wa be still sleep *a a*
wa wa wa be still sleep *a a*
wa wa wa wa be still sleep *a a*
wa wa wa wa be still sleep *a*
  o

CROW SONG

for Tetsuo Nagasawa

take my hands, Crow, a little dirt & blood on them
    but I give you my hands—
my lungs & chest, take the air I breathe, all its smells
    sweet grass, rain on the ground
I give you my head, all that I remember, all that I know
    (lean pickings?)
take my belly then, Crow, nuts & berries & meat in it
    I give you my belly
my mouth, I give you my mouth—
    (what'll you do with my mouth?)
I give you my feet, my legs, they carry me well—
    they've always been good to me
you can have my eyes, Crow, they're as good as yours
    I give you my eyes
my rattling tongue, I give you my tongue
    cedarbark or your own is smoother
I give you my ears, what do they hear?
    I can hear mice in green grass
have my blood, Crow, it's still warm
    I'll give you my blood
my meat, not too tender, call it well-aged
    I give you my meat
all that I am—I give you myself
    all there is of me

Can you hear? You there? Or do I sing to myself?

I could've offered you anything—
    you want my doubts & fears?

I give you what I have
I'll give you my dreams, I have fine dreams
I'll give you what I wish I had
    (& what I never wanted)
I give it all to you, Crow
everything
    whether I know what it's all about or not
    whether I can follow the tracks or not

you can have the rivers, banks falling in, sandbars shifting
    who knows where they're deep or shallow
& take the darkness, night, the stars are too far away
  & the woods too dark
    (& the rivers talk at night)
    take the moon too
take all my black prattle, yap yap yap
my standing around, sitting around

all my trails grown over with blackberries
my springs muddied, or dried up
& the wind is too cold for my clothes
& there's too much snow
my tongue is old leather—all the oils gone out of it—
I've seen the nighthawks roll in the dust
I've tired of the children's play

What do you say, Crow? Do I see the shadows of your wings?

Crow, what's mine is yours—it always was

it always was—but I'm still using it

O Crow, I'm still using everything I have

O Crow, maybe I'm a crow too

Crow & Alive

alive when I sleep, alive awake—HAH, Crow
alive when I dance
alive when I sing—I sing loud & well, of myself, my troubles,
                                                    my joys
alive when I dance
I burn in my own fires

I'M ALIVE IF I ONLY WATCH

ALIVE

the night's alive & dances with me
I'm keeping it all. I am it all
I'll sing Life for whoever wants to hear it—

ALIVE ALIVE ALIVE

    CAN YOU HEAR ME, CROW???

      HAH! HAH! HAH!!!

We change to keep all else the same

Crows fill the tree, get up
one by one, heavy, together
swing black across the blue
settle, one by one
together, fill the leafless tree

I burn six candles
white candles on a white plate

six deer, dark in the snow, their heads
turned to me, & hawks
wheel above me, blue sky
the deer do not move

Your hair has turned to Magpie feathers

Mars, opalescent orange, McIbbon's crystal ball
   reflects fire light
the sheen of ten brass shells whirring
she swings them over her very blond head

we dance as the moon disappears
howl & hoot dance drum
the orange moon disappears

she asks for a boy but I
bring none
she asks for a girl but I
only smile
          she writhes on her back
comes & comes
          hears us

we fuck in high oat grass
children in a circle around us

   "Here the world ends, here
  it begins. I fly between. Bring word
    after the beginning, before the end."

wide wings thru dark trees

all that he could catch of her was white light
    & the black behind

owl, just returned from the dead

    "I wasn't really there"

the deer, out of the trees, downhill
the lake below, slowly, one foot
then another, down the dozed road

I had heard of her beauty

three hawks, low, crows below them
a calf, trying to stand
placenta still swinging from the cow

I caught her eyes

the owl, out of the trees
turns, returns
no place to come down

*All through the night they rode
circled the Pole Star*

      *blue white yellow & red ribbons
an iron bell before me*

next to the cedar stood an oak
—the road ran between them—
I hung a rope from the oak, climbed it
could see more of the mountain—gold—in the north

the goat—Thunder—was killed at harvest
the dog ate her heart

we filled the room with hemp smoke—owl claws & feathers
outside, I looked into the dog's eyes
saw a dead man under the cedar

the blond woman came down from the mountains
watched over the child's birth

drunk, I pulled on a string of blue beads & iron bells
rung them—the bottom bell came off in my hand
I walked ahead, the road muddy in heavy rain
she followed, baby bundled in her arms
the wind louder than the rain where we came into the trees

where we'd watched for deer, along the river
the bell before me, a woman
crashed, killed herself
thrown from her car, her body under my truck

I found spotted mushrooms under the cedar

found a fox dead in the road—traded her skin
for the spotted feather of a golden eagle

with blue white yellow & red ribbons
I tied three sheep skulls high in the oak
at dusk with iron pots for drums
I sang a circle around the house & down the road

at midnight—the roar of a single motorcycle
then another & another—thirteen riders
beer to fill the bed of a truck
we sang, ran berserk, raced
all night over the dark hills—into & out of the flames
the best rider of them all fell into the coals
we pulled him out—unburned—put him to bed
he slept until dusk, was the last to leave

the child grew, one summer night squealed for joy
the iron pots rang where they hung
& the riders came again
burned their fire, all of the wood
in the morning one of them pierced the child's ears

when we left the place, he had returned
stood with the others in the road, waved after us

rounding a curve, far to the east
a golden eagle flew up before us

WIND
Fragments for a beginning

eyes & tongue & before me the tree from which I sing
when sung to
no song without me, no song
unless I pull myself into the tree
let those words wing through me

Thunder & Lightning & Wind

I cut my drum from a lightning struck tree
ride the roar & crash flash & roll

feathers fly
eagle & owl lift in the wind

———————————

we are the Wind
people of the Horse & Wheel & Blue Sky

we named all the rivers
from the marshes below Rainbow Bridge
to the sea that turns to salt
Salmon swim for us

we named Birch & Beech & Oak & Willow
Bear Wolf & Wasp

        we are the Wind
our people gather in the groves where lightning lives
        our tents open to the unmoving star

---

        what the Sun allows
        the battles won, the deeds done
        we make promises for
        we will hang by our arms, chest or back
        we hang for the Sun

        the chosen virgin, with never used axe
        fells the chosen Birch
        strips it of all branches but two
        a cross near the top
        all virgins carry the tree
        to where it is set, upright, in the ground

        the horse's skull is placed, faced to the east
        a spear sunk slanting over the skull, to the tree

        our tents circle the tree
        the circle open to the east

        those who will hang
        fast for three nights
        & when the Sun rises
        a direct line, Sun to spear & skull to tree
        their skin is pierced
        strips of hide tied to the uncut limbs
        pulled through the pierced skin
        drawn tight, they hang
        the hide pulls out if they fall
        if they stand, their skin is cut
        when they are ready

rubbed with healing salve

when all are free
babies are laid down
bundled in fur, around the tree
their ears pierced
the furs are left
taken by those who need them

we feast, & those without
leave their spears before a tent
& the host of their choosing feeds them

---

when we first rode down
they told us there was no place to graze

they didn't want us to build our fires
said their fields would catch

they had everything all tore up
mud walls all over the place
all the game run off

they were eating grass

all them people living together
trying to make ends without moving
when we first saw them
we knew there wasn't room for all of us

---

         we rode through their fields
         rode to their mud walled towns
         long haired, our faces painted red
         our horses deer headed, deer horned
         we shook our spears, swung our axes
               wolves ran behind us

            Tuwaz rode to the wall
         threw his spear over the wall
         threw back his head & laughed
         raised his one arm & yelled

               We are the Wind
         We made dust of your fields
         We will make dust of your walls
             nothing stands before us
               We are the Wind

         _____

our hair grows long
until we kill

when we marry
a man gives his wife weapons
& she gives him tools
men & women fight & work

we gather armed
sword & spear & axe
all have their say
our plans made
disagreements talked out

all acts weighed, just & unjust
payments are made

we destroy the swords, all things
of traitors & cowards
cut off their heads
sink them in the swamps

---

when the days are short
when our fingers & toes freeze, & snow
stays long on the ground
when the nights are longest
we give to the sky

we hang deer & pig
whatever we have
one hung the first day
two the second
three the third
until seventy-eight hang

then we burn them, feast
& the days grow longer
the nights shorter

---

we divide the land we use
each year, choose lots
keep what we raise

when we build houses
they are small, spread out
a man, his wife & children live alone

when callers come we feed them
if all we have, we go to another's house
& he will feed us all

---

naked & wrapped in hawk skins
she told of flying, we feasted
flew with her

she rolled through all their lands, in the spring
in her wagon, covered
in the wagon, they all thought
it had to do with their crops coming up
o fuck me, she said
until she tired, bathed for days in the sea

she was part of the bargain
we sent two men & they sent her
one of the two we sent was stupid
& they thought we'd tricked them
killed him, sent us his skull

she dried the mushrooms, soaked them in milk
we all drank & feasted
she fluttered her wings, told of flying
o fuck me, she said, & we did
rolled with her, feathers & all
o we flew

it all had to do with their crops
didn't have anything to do with us

the old woman strangled her

we burned her, gave her to the sky

>   we drove off some of their cows
>   kept them with ours
>   in one of the hill corrals
>
>   the night before they came
>   we'd feasted, were all laid out
>   that damn bitch, with her magic milk
>   only Tuwaz was awake, heard them coming
>
>   he tried to wake us, but couldn't
>   sometimes we slept for days
>   we couldn't help him, & he
>   walked out alone, met them in the meadow
>
>   All my people, he called
>   tried to chain the wolf we keep
>   I chained him, though he took my arm
>   I am the bravest of my people
>   Send your bravest to me, your wolves
>   let them try for the other arm
>
>   their leader called his favorites forward
>   one by one, & Tuwaz met them
>   cut them down, laughing, set their heads in a row
>   until their leader would send no more
>   & they turned, went home without their cows

>   when he is killed
>   a man's things are divided
>   a third for his family
>   a third for his feast
>   a third goes with him

a wooden tent is built over him
covered with dirt
sometimes circled with stones
if he is not burned

Tuwaz burned, & not alone
all the women wanted to go with him

his horse went down
& they remembered him
swarmed over him
& we lost many bringing him home

he had many horses, & cattle
like one of their kings
his wife & children were rich
with only their third
& the feast lasted for days
the women to go with him
drunk out of their minds
fucking all who would have them

it was something to see
twelve horses & six of the women

the flames reached to the sky

I sat in the sky
the eagle sat with me
Wind spoke to me
& Lightning & Thunder

they thought he was stupid, listen to him

crows on each of my shoulders
nine days in the tree
nine days, & I returned

even the wolf listens

Printed July 1976 in Santa Barbara & Ann Arbor for the Black Sparrow Press by Mackintosh & Young and Edwards Brothers Inc. Design by Barbara Martin. This edition is published in paper wrappers; there are 200 hardcover copies numbered & signed by the author; & 26 lettered copies handbound in boards by Earle Gray each containing an original holograph poem by James Koller.

Photo: M. Swift

Born in 1936 in Oak Park, Illinois, James Koller now lives in Georgetown, Maine. Since 1964 he has edited *Coyote's Journal* and Coyote Books, first in San Francisco and later in New Mexico and Maine. His first book of poems, *Two Hands: Poems 1959-1961* was published in 1965. He has since authored numerous books of poetry, including *The Dogs & Other Dark Woods* (Four Seasons, 1966), *Some Cows* (Coyote Books, 1966), and *California Poems* (Black Sparrow, 1971).

Koller has travelled extensively throughout the United States, spending most of his time west of the Rockies and in the Northeast. In 1968 and again in 1973 he was awarded a grant from the National Endowment for the Arts.